ONE HUNDRED WAYS A

Horse is Better Than a Man

D0696165

ALSO BY TINA BETTISON:

100 Ways for a Horse to Train Its Human

100 Ways to Live with a Horse Addict

ONE HUNDRED WAYS A

*Horse is Better
Than a Man*

BY
Tina Bettison

ILLUSTRATIONS BY
Åsa Andersson

HODDER

Text Copyright © 2007 by Tina Bettison
Illustrations Copyright © 2007 by Åsa Andersson

First published in Great Britain in 2007

The right of Tina Bettison to be identified as the Author of
the Work has been asserted by her in accordance with the
Copyright, Designs and Patents Act 1988.

1

British Library Cataloguing in Publication Data
A record for this book is available from the British Library

ISBN 978 0340 943526

Printed in the UK by CPI Bookmarque,
Croydon, CR0 4TD

The paper and board used in this paperback are natural
recyclable products made from wood grown in sustainable
forests. The manufacturing processes conform to the
environmental regulations of the country of origin.

Hodder & Stoughton
A Division of Hodder Headline Ltd
338 Euston Road
London NW1 3BH
www.madaboutbooks.com

For all the men who are, and
will be, in the lives of women
with horses. You are all
adorable but the horses will
always come first.
Just accept it.

$\mathcal{C}$ontents

Introduction

Both Men and horses are beautiful creatures and they each have advantages and merits. But the battle of the sexes will always rage on because men and women just have different ways of looking at the world. And so for many women, if it comes down to the choice of horse or husband, the horse wins every time. These 100 ways are just a few of the reasons why!

Relationships

Horses don't think you are boring if you want a night in with a face pack and a bottle of wine to watch your favourite soap.

Horses are never impressed by other women's breasts and don't feel a need to ask if they are real.

Horses may give other women attention, but only for as long as they have food. They quickly lose interest once they have eaten the mints.

Even if you look longingly at another horse and wish yours could do what he can do, you never stop loving your own.

Y ou just know your horse is The One and even if he isn't, you can always keep him AND have another one or two.

H orses don't need reassurance that you prefer them to George Clooney, Brad Pitt or Sean Connery (still sexy in his 70s, yum!!). Nor do they worry about whether you fancy the horse next door.

Cute and handsome horses don't keep checking themselves in the puddles to make sure they are still cute and handsome.

If your horse trots off with your best friend, it's with your blessing. In fact a spot of horse swapping is positively encouraged to improve your own riding, and experience the feel of different beasts.

Horses don't get frustrated if you can't understand the offside rule, the point of cricket or why rugby players are constantly having a group hug.

Excitable horses can be kept on a tight rein and if necessary turned in circles until they calm down.

Your horse won't begrudge the time you spend doing things without him, like retail therapy or nights out with the girls.

You will always forgive your horse for forgetting your birthday or anniversary.

If you say 'we need to talk about our relationship' to a horse, he won't run off.

The word 'commitment' doesn't frighten a horse, it just means he agrees to let you ride him in return for food.

If the relationship with your horse doesn't work out you can sell it or shoot it and neither will result in your arrest.

If your horse can no longer fulfil the purpose for which you got it, you might be able to claim loss of use from your insurance.

Your horse won't end the relationship with the old chestnut 'it's not you, it's me!'

Horses don't go bald or grow beer bellies, or still think they're attractive when they've done both.

Horses only ever wear what you dress them in. No matter how bizarre and eclectic your tastes, they'll just wear that latest-fashion rug anyway. Their only contribution to their attire is mud.

Your horse does not begrudge the time you spend with him and will happily while away the hours with you, especially if there are mints or carrots for sharing.

Horses don't help themselves to your cash, though they are very good at helping you spend it.

Horses don't get insecure if you earn more than they do – it just means more hay.

You never have to hide a new purchase in your wardrobe or tack room for three weeks – pretending you've had it for ages – before showing it to your horse.

You never look at your horse and wonder if you still love him; or what happened to that handsome young colt you fell for all those years ago.

Communication

Horses don't always think you're right, but they don't always have to prove you're wrong either.

Horses won't criticise your driving or your parking capabilities but they may become difficult to load if they object to your cornering technique.

Your horse won't laugh and call you a silly cow if you reverse into a lamppost.

If your horse isn't happy in the relationship he'll tell you; you don't need to spend hours wondering what's wrong and trying to analyse his every word to work it out.

You'll never get into an argument with your horse because he won't stop to ask directions. He will always implicitly trust your map reading and sense of direction. If in doubt, he'll just head for the juiciest grass and stay there until you've sorted it out.

Horses don't point out the spot you've been trying to cover up, the hair colour that didn't quite match the packet or the fact that your jeans look a bit tight. And they'll never give you the wrong answer to 'Does my bum look big in this?'

Horses look to you to take the leadership role in the relationship and are really happy when you do.

H orses know how to listen (or at least they know how to look as though they are listening!).

You never refuse to play with your horse because it's getting too competitive.

Horses make it very clear when they want to go out; they don't bother with concocted excuses, they just bang on the door!

Horses know what 'NO' means, though they still might ignore you.

Horses don't change the subject just because they don't want to have *that* conversation.

Horses usually look at you when you are talking to them; and if not, it's quite easy to get their attention with a carrot.

Horses make it quite clear if they don't like another horse; they don't feign politeness then mutter under their breath.

It's very obvious when your horse is jealous; it's that ears pinned back, eye-rolling snarl with bared teeth aimed at the object of their jealousy that gives it away. Men have been known to adopt that expression too, of course.

Apparently we women speak an average of 40,000 words a day, whereas men only speak about 10,000. Your horse will be quite happy for you to natter away and use up your excess words, without trying to interrupt or fix the problem that you just wanted to air.

Neither horses nor men speak the same language as women but horses are just much easier to understand. Horses say what they mean, and mean what they say!

Horses ask sensible questions like 'Is that a monster?' when they see a plastic bag in the hedge; or 'Is that what you wanted?' as they buck excitedly when you ask for a canter transition.

Horses don't feel the need to prove their prowess by jumping higher, running faster or eating more hay than another horse. *We* might feel the need to prove their prowess, but that's another matter.

Your horse won't pretend to know about a subject when he hasn't a clue, just to impress other horses.

Horses have incredible patience. No matter how many times you get something wrong, they'll wait for you to get it right and then reward you by perfectly performing the very thing you were trying to ask for.

Your horse rarely objects to being groomed, even while eating.

If you're talking to your horse he won't constantly try to define every word you say or take everything literally, then try to get one over on you by insisting his opinion is the correct one and he has scientific evidence to prove it.

Horses can take several instructions at once and cope. If you give more than one instruction at the same time to a man, his brain explodes – this, apparently, is because he's from Mars. Does this mean horses must be from Venus too?

Ailments and Mare-ish Behaviour

We all know that there is nothing worse than a man with an ailment (except, of course, a woman with PMT).

When your horse feels a bit unwell, he will let you know but won't bang on for weeks about his near-death experience with the common cold.

Your horse does not need to compete with you over who is the sickest and feels the worst, particularly if a cold happens to strike you both together. He also won't blame you for passing it on.

You don't have to share the TV with a horse, so you can watch weepies in peace with as much chocolate as you like.

When your horse is poorly you'll willingly sleep in the stable with him.

If your horse is on bed rest, you can occupy him with hay and leave him to amuse himself.

When you have to play nurse and change dressings, you can sedate your horse to avoid being kicked.

A male horse doesn't know what PMT is and, no matter how grumpy you are, will still love you. He will forgive most moods and, unless you have been unnecessarily violent and abusive, won't hold a grudge or bring up your mood swings in every discussion for the next twenty years.

Horses can be chucked out in a field when you want some personal space and they really don't mind.

51

Mares may not label it PMT, but they know what it feels like. You can understand your mare's seasonal mood swings too. You know just how she feels. There is comfort to be drawn from this shared experience.

You don't have to justify to your horse why you need a whole set of jodphurs a size larger than you usually wear to accommodate that 'time of the month' bloat.

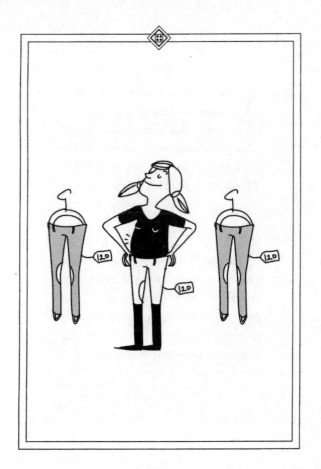

Your horse won't steal your stash of medicinal chocolate and then accuse you of over reacting when you politely point out that you NEEDED THAT CHOCOLATE NOW!!!!!

When you feel that PMT low, your horse will always give you a hug and a nuzzle, and remind you of just how special you are. Some may try to suggest that the horse is merely wiping his nose on you, but you know what it really means.

The Mating Game

Horses don't cancel dates at the last minute with lame excuses. *You* cancel the date with *them* when they really are lame.

You can leave a horse alone in the stable while you go out on the town and he won't object to you rolling home drunk with another horse's number written on your arm.

Men have this strange habit of being all over you like a rash at the early stages of a relationship and then treating you like a rash when you have finally succumbed to their charms. Horses take time to get to know you well before lavishing you with their affections. You know where you are with a horse.

If you have an overwhelming desire to ride your best friend's horse she'll probably let you.

Horses can't go shopping, which is a double-edged sword: they can't buy you that nice Tiffany necklace you hanker after (and you just *know* that they would if they could), but then they won't buy you a state of the art, practical and useful power drill either.

Horses don't actually care what you are wearing as long as there are treats in the pocket; and they are rarely fazed by long leather boots and a schooling whip.

Horses are better at foreplay; they will happily nuzzle you for hours, as long as you have mints in your pocket.

Horses are not at all bothered when you don't want to ride them and you never have to fake a headache as an excuse. Equally, you can ride them whenever you like, for as long as you like, even while the football is on.

If your stallion is getting to be too much of a handful you can have his testicles removed to calm him down and make him more compliant. Men seem to object to this.

You don't ever have to sleep with your horse, unless you really want to . . .

You always know that as long as you have shut the stable door, your horse will stay put. Occasionally you might get one who can undo bolts and you'll find him on the nearest patch of green grass. It might be the horse equivalent of heaving cleavage, but it is easily tempted back with a juicy carrot and hay net.

If another woman says to your horse, 'Hello big boy, you're lovely; can I stroke you?' you feel really quite proud and not at all threatened!

DIY and Other Strange Male Obsessions

Why is it that when we put men and DIY together, it always seems to lead to frustration. With a horse, you never have to worry about DIY disasters, and you can pay a man who can, rather than get p****d off with a man who can't!

A horse will very quickly tell you if he is capable of a job and won't keep pretending he can when he can't. He won't insist on fixing his own stable door and then not get round to it.

Your horse won't get huffy when you suggest getting a professional in.

Horses don't have a need to take things apart to see how they work and then not be able to put them back together.

You don't have to feign an interest in your horse's main hobby of grazing to maintain a good relationship with him or have something you can both talk about.

Horses don't moan at how many pairs of shoes you have in the wardrobe and then go and buy yet another gadget, which just adds to the pile in the tool shed. At least you know the only gadgets your horse has are the absolutely necessary paraphernalia that you bought on a retail therapy spree.

Horses do not become obsessive about incomprehensible things such as pressure washers, power drills, vintage tractors, or buying utterly useless things from eBay. They become obsessive about sensible things like mints and carrots.

When you have a horse, you will never be a golf widow nor spend Saturdays alone while your man tinkers with his 'toys'.

Horses do not get hooked on Sudoku puzzles or any other latest craze and spend hours locked in a world of their own playing them. Though it's probably a blessing that men do; it leaves us free to play with the horses!

Family and Friends

You won't have to meet your horse's parents before you commit to each other, nor will you ever have to spend Christmas with them.

It's unlikely that any of his family members will appear on your doorstep when you weren't expecting them. And you certainly won't have to put up with his arrogant brother or flighty sister (unless you bred all three of them!).

Horses may not be happy to see your family, but they never pass comment, beyond perhaps a small nip. They certainly don't go on about your mother.

Horses are not embarrassed by public displays of affection. You can pet them as much as you like, when you like, anywhere you like and they won't wriggle or turn crimson. Even your aunty Mavis can descend on them with puckered lips and they won't bat an eyelid.

His mother will never think you aren't good enough for him and voice her opinion at every opportunity.

You never have to choose the right moment to tell your horse that your mother is coming to stay . . . for a month.

Horses don't expect you to impress, entertain or even talk to their friends. And you never find them hung over, littering your lounge in the morning.

Horses don't bring their loud, smelly friends round to your house to watch *Horse of the Year* show.

Horses don't complain about your friends or how much time you spend on the phone to them.

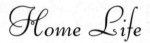

Home Life

Horses don't need to be house trained. Mucking out their stable gives you valuable thinking time and saves a trip to the gym. Picking up men's undies does neither.

You can keep your horse on full livery and let someone else do all the work; and if you find her in his bed, you know it's all part of the service.

Horses think everything you feed them is delicious and usually wolf it down with gusto.

If your horse has behavioural problems, you can usually get some sort of calming supplement or, failing that, a horse whisperer to retrain him.

If your horse snores and farts in his sleep, it really doesn't matter.

Horses will usually greet you with an enthusiastic nicker. Men often greet you with a grunt. They both mean 'what's for dinner?' but somehow it is so much more endearing coming from a horse.

Horses don't mind if you put on a little weight, though they might object to carrying too many extra kilos.

You can feed a horse the same thing day after day for weeks on end, so you never have to agonise over what to cook for his dinner.

Your horse might not miss you when you are gone, but he won't need to moan for half an hour about the day he had in the field when you come back.

At the end of a long day you know your horse will always be there, with a warm hug and a nuzzle, and he'll let you bury your nose in his neck for as long as you like – as long as he's fed and watered. Just like a man!